Angry Birds
Bad Piggies' Egg Recipes

Illustration & layout by Pasi Pitkänen
Graphic design by Pasi Pitkänen & Mikko Hiltunen
Pre-press design by Anne-Marie Vesto
Pre-press editing by Jackie Alpers
Written by Bonnier Kirjat Oy

ISBN 978-952-276-000-5

Printed in Canada

TABLE OF CONTENTS

EGGSPERT

EGG MAGIC

EGGSTRAS

GOOD OL' TIMES
EGG SALAD

Serves two piggies:

- 1/3 head of leaf lettuce
- 2 eggs
- 1 cucumber

Dressing:

- 1/4 cup of mayonnaise
- 1/4 cup of sour cream
- 1 teaspoon of lemon juice
- 1/2 teaspoon of sugar
- white pepper and chili powder to taste
- 1/2 teaspoon of sweet mustard

 Hard boil the eggs (see instructions on page 17). Put them in a bowl of ice water to help them cool down before cracking the shells and separating the egg whites and the yolk.

2. Slice up the lettuce, cucumber and egg whites and place them in a bowl. Chop the yolks into small pieces and sprinkle on top of the salad.

3. Prepare the dressing by mixing the rest of the ingredients. Pour the dressing on the salad or keep it separate according to your preference.

YAMMY SAMMY
EGG SALAD SANDWICH

For one piggy:

- 1 hard-boiled egg
- 1–2 tablespoons of mayonnaise
- 2 tablespoons of chopped celery
- 1 tablespoon of chopped green onion
- curry powder
- salt and pepper
- 1 leaf of lettuce
- 2 slices of dark rye bread

 Chop the egg by using a fork (just a bit, don't mash it to pulp). Mix the onion, celery, mayonnaise and egg together. Season with salt, pepper and curry powder. Mix it all together.

2. Toast the bread. Place a layer of lettuce on one slice, spread egg mixture on top and close the deal with another slice of toasted bread.

THE EASY ONE
SCRAMBLED EGGS

For two hungry medium size pigs:

- *6 large eggs (NOT ostrich size!)*
- *6 teaspoons of low-fat milk*
- *1 tablespoon of butter/oil*
- *spices (usually salt & pepper)*

 1. Take a large frying pan, heat it up and add the butter/oil.

 2. In the meantime, take a bowl, whisk the eggs with milk.

3. Use a spatula and push the eggs towards the center until no running parts are visible. At this point you flip the egg mixture over. Wait for 30 seconds and voilá.

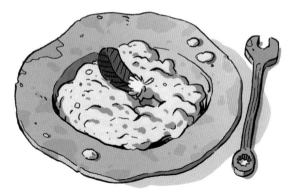

THE ARRIVISTE'S CHOICE
BOILED EGGS AND FRIED EGGS

BOILED EGGS

1. Place eggs in a medium saucepan; add cold water to cover by 1 inch. Bring to rolling boil. Remove pan from heat; cover, and let stand 13 minutes for hard-cooked eggs and 6 minutes for soft-cooked eggs.

2. After boiling, pour the hot water out and add cold water into the pan. Let the eggs stand in cold water until they are cool enough to handle.

FRIED EGGS

3. For eggs sunny-side up, warm a small amount of oil or butter (1 1/2 tsp.) in a small skillet over medium heat. Crack an egg into the pan and cook until the white has set (3 to 4 minutes). Serve. For completely fried eggs, flip the egg over after 2 to 3 min and cook another minute or two. Voilá!

THE SURVIVOR'S CHOICE
OMELET

For one superior pig:

- 3 large eggs
- 1 tablespoon of milk
- 1 tablespoon of butter/oil
- salt (to season)

The filling can be anything from vegetables to meat or a mixture of both.

 Separate the yolks from the whites, beat them separately and then mix them together – this is to add volume to the texture. Add the milk and beat shortly.

 Heat the pan over medium-low heat until the butter or oil sizzles. Pour the mixture into the hot pan. When the eggs start to set, gently push them away from the edge of the pan with a spatula. Tilt the pan so that the egg that is still wet will fill in the bottom of the pan. The eggs should still be moist before adding the filling. Spread the filling down the center.

Fold the omelet in half by lifting one side up and flipping it over the filling to match the opposite side. Turn off the heat and cover the pan with a lid. Let the omelet sit for a couple of minutes.

According to your preference you can continue to cook the omelet a bit longer until the center is fully set. (Brush a dash of melted butter on top, thus giving a pretty and professional look to the omelet and adding some extra flavor.)

OMELET ACCIDENTE
BACON/HAM OMELET

Add some ham or bacon (1/4 pound). Slice and/or dice the precooked meat and add on top of the omelet when the eggs are not set yet. Remember that you don't have to add salt if the meat is salted.

RAINBOW
BELL PEPPER OMELET

Dice some green, red and yellow bell peppers (1/3 per pepper), fry quickly over medium heat with a bit of oil before adding the egg mixture as in a regular omelet.

OMELET FILIPINO
CHICKEN OMELET

Add some chicken (1/8 pound) and rice (1/8 pound). Fry/cook the chicken and cook the rice according to the instructions if they are not precooked. Dice the chicken and mix with rice in a bowl. Place on top of one half of the almost ready omelet. Flip the other side on the "toppings", creating a pouch. Serve with saffron and ketchup.

CARAMBA!
BURRITO

Four servings:

- 2 tablespoons of olive oil
- 8 small potatoes
- 1/2 pound of chorizo sausage, sliced
- 8 to 10-inch flour tortillas
- 1 tablespoon of butter
- 5 eggs
- 4 ounces of cream cheese
- 3 tablespoons of chopped cilantro
- 1/4 cup of green salsa
- 1 tablespoon of chili powder
- salt and ground black pepper to taste

 Preheat the oven to 200°F. Heat olive oil in a large skillet. Slice the potatoes and place in the skillet; season with salt, pepper and chili powder. Cook until potatoes are tender (approx. 10 minutes). Place on a baking sheet and put in the preheated oven.

 Stir chorizo into skillet and cook until browned and crumbly. Pour the grease out. Place the chorizo in the oven with the potatoes for some minutes. Cover the tortillas with aluminum foil and place in the warm oven.

 Melt butter in a clean skillet. Break the eggs into the skillet and stir while cooking. When the eggs are nearly set, mix in the chorizo and potatoes. Add the cream cheese and stir until melted. Fold in the cilantro just before serving.

4. Take one tortilla at a time. Spoon the fillings onto the lower half. Fold the sides over the filling, and then roll the tortillas into a tight cylinder. Top with green salsa to serve.

FIRE IN THE HOLE

Create a hotter filling by adding one or two habanero chilies, sliced and squashed.

HUFFIN 'N' PUFFIN

CHEESE AND EGG SOUFFLÉ

For one medium size pig:

- *4 egg whites*
- *1 teaspoon of corn starch*
- *3 tablespoons of butter*
- *3 tablespoons of all-purpose flour*
- *1 cup of milk*
- *1/2 cup of freshly grated Parmesan cheese*
- *salt to taste*
- *dash of nutmeg*

1. Start by melting butter in a pan. Then add flour and start stirring until the mixture is smooth. Add 1/4 cup of milk and continue stirring until the mixture thickens.

2. Pour the remaining milk into the sticky mixture gradually and continue to cook and stir.

3. When the mixture is smooth and thick, add the cheese and seasonings. Continue cooking and stirring until everything is well combined. Remove from heat and refrigerate until cool.

 4. Using an electric mixer, beat the egg whites and corn starch on low until foamy. Then increase the speed to high until they form stiff peaks.

5. Fold one fourth of the egg whites into the cheese mixture with a rubber spatula. When it's fully mixed in, gently fold in the rest of the egg whites.

 6. Grease a 7-inch soufflé dish with butter and dust with parmesan cheese. Spoon the soufflé mixture into the dish. Before putting it in the oven, use a spatula to make the top look like a dome.

7. Put the dish into the preheated oven (375°F), slightly above the center for 25 to 35 minutes minutes. Don't open the door for the first 20 minutes. The soufflé is ready when it is puffed and brown.

LIFT ME UP
ZUCCHINI OMELET

Serves four:

- 4 eggs
- 2 tablespoons of Parmesan cheese
- 2 tablespoons of olive oil
- 1 zucchini
- 1 clove of garlic
- salt and black pepper

1. Beat the eggs lightly in a bowl. Add the grated cheese, stir and set aside. Slice the zucchini to 1/8 to 1/4-inch thick pieces.

2. Heat the olive oil in a skillet and cook the zucchini slices until softened and lightly browned (takes about 7 minutes).

3. Season the zucchini with squashed garlic, add some salt and pepper for taste. Reduce the heat to medium and pour the egg mixture into the skillet.

4. Cook for 2 to 3 minutes, stirring gently. Remove the skillet from the heat. Cover skillet and keep covered until the eggs set (approx. 3 minutes).

BIG BOY
GIANT SQUARE OMELET

For the whole neighborhood :

- 5 leeks
- 5 tablespoons of cooking oil
- 5 1/2 pounds of asparagus
- 1 pint of fresh herbs (e.g. basil)
- 30 eggs
- 1/2 cup of cream
- 9 ounces of grated cheese
- 5 teaspoons of salt
- 1 1/4 teaspoon of black pepper
- parsley

 Preheat the oven to 350°F. Chop the white parts of the leeks and fry them in a pan with oil until they are golden brown.

 Cook the asparagus in salted water for 3 minutes. When done, dry the asparagus with paper towels before cutting into 1-inch pieces. Crush the fresh herbs. Spread the ingredients evenly into a buttered baking sheet (or large jelly roll pan).

 Break the eggs into a bowl and mix evenly after adding the cream. Add the grated cheese. Season and pour the mixture evenly onto the baking sheet.

Bake for 30 minutes or until the omelet has set and its surface is golden brown. Let it cool for a few minutes before cutting and lifting the pieces. Sprinkle some fresh parsley on top before serving.

SHAKE 'EM!
CHOCOLATE SHAKE

One per piggy:

- *2 cups of vanilla ice cream*
- *1/2 cup of milk*
- *1/4 cup of powdered chocolate drink mix*
- *1 egg white**

Combine the ice cream, milk, chocolate drink mix and egg white in a blender. Blend until smooth. Just to make sure the mixture gets evenly mixed, stir once or twice with a spoon.

If you are going to or coming from the gym, you might want to add some powdered protein mix to the shake. (In this case, be sure to add some extra milk so your shake doesn't get too thick.)

BANANA ALTERNATIVE:

- 1 banana
- 1 tablespoon of lemon juice
- 4 tablespoons of white sugar
- 1 cup of milk
- 1 cup of plain yogurt
- 1/4 cup of whipped cream
- 1 egg white*

Pour the fruit (sliced/chopped banana, apple etc.), lemon juice and sugar in the blender. Blend until smooth. Add the milk, egg white and yogurt and blend for another minute. Pour the mixture into a glass and top the beauty with a dab of whipped cream.

VANILLA ALTERNATIVE:

- 2 cups of juice
- 2 scoops of vanilla ice cream
- 1 egg white*

Combine the ingredients in a blender. Blend until smooth.

*RAW EGG WARNING!

CHEESY DREAM
CHEESECAKE

Serves 12 piggies:

The crust:
- *1 cup of graham cracker crumbs (about 8 whole crackers smashed fine)*
- *1 tablespoon of granulated sugar*
- *5 tablespoons of butter, melted*

The filling:
- *2 1/2 pounds of cream cheese, softened*
- *1 3/4 cups of granulated sugar*
- *3 tablespoons of all-purpose flour*
- *5 eggs and 2 egg yolks*
- *1/4 cup of heavy whipping cream*

1. Lightly coat a 10-inch springform pan with oil. In a bowl, combine the ingredients for the crust. Press mixture to the edges of the pan. Bake for 15 minutes at 325°F. Let cool.

2. In a large bowl, combine the cream cheese, sugar, flour, eggs and egg yolks and mix thoroughly. Then add cream and mix only enough to blend. Pour filling over crust and bake for 10 minutes at 475°F. Reduce temperature to 200°F and continue to bake for 1 hour.

3. Turn the oven off, but leave the cake in for another hour. Let the cake chill overnight in the refrigerator.

KILL THE COOK
EGGS DELMONICO

**Serves two minions
or one working pig:**

- *10 1/2 ounces of condensed cream
  of mushroom soup*
- *1/2 cup of cheddar cheese*
- *4 hard-boiled eggs*
- *1 tablespoon of pimiento peppers*
- *toast*
- *paprika*

Heat the soup in a pan over medium heat for
3 to 5 minutes or until it starts bubbling. In the
meantime, shred the cheese, slice the eggs and chop
the pimiento. Reduce the heat to low and stir in the
cheese. Stir until cheese is melted.

Fold in eggs and pimiento, heat for two minutes.
Place on toast and sprinkle some paprika on top
for color and taste.

GRILLED DELIGHT
GRILLED EGGS

**Serves four
bad piggies:**

- *10 eggs*

1. Fire up an outdoor grill (outdoors, please).

2. Use a muffin pan: coat all cups with cooking spray and break one egg per cup. Try to keep the yolks intact for a nice presentation.

3. Place the pan on the grill and cook for 2–3 minutes over medium heat.

4. Serve with mixed vegetables/salad.

OVEN MADE
OVEN EGGS

Serves two piggies:

- *2 teaspoons of cream*
- *2 eggs*
- *1 teaspoon of minced chives*
- *salt and pepper to taste*
- *grated cheese*
- *butter*

1. Preheat the oven to 325°F. Grease the inside of a ramekin with some butter. Pour the cream on the bottom of the ramekin.

2. Break the eggs on top of the cream without damaging the yolks. Add salt, pepper, chives and grated cheese. Bake for 12 to 15 minutes or until the whites have set (the yolks are still soft). Remove from oven and allow to set for 2 to 3 minutes before serving.

EGGAMANIAC | 33

SAUCE GENERALLISSIMA
EGG SAUCE

For two servings:

- *1 tablespoon of butter*
- *1 tablespoon of flour*
- *3/4 cup of milk*
- *1 hard-boiled egg*
- *1/4 teaspoon of salt*
- *1/8 teaspoon of black pepper*

 Melt the butter in a small saucepan. Mix in the flour, salt and pepper. Cook over low heat. Stir until mixture is smooth. Remove from heat and stir in milk.

2. Heat to boiling. Then, stir the mixture constantly for one minute. Dice the egg and add to the mixture. Serve with boiled potatoes.

GALLIC GARLIC
AIOLI SAUCE

For four:

- *5 cloves of garlic*
- *2 egg yolks*
- *1 cup plus 1 tablespoon of olive oil*
- *1 1/2 tablespoons of lemon juice*
- *salt and pepper*

1. Peel the garlic cloves and crush them in a mortar with some salt and a tablespoon of oil.

2. Pour the mixture in a blender and add the egg yolks and rest of the oil while blending.

3. Season with salt and pepper and finish off with lemon juice. Serve with seafood or boiled vegetables.

ICE, ICE BABY
SORBET

10 to 12 servings:

- *1 cup of water or wine*
- *1/2 cup of sugar*
- *1 1/2 cups of berries*
- *2 egg whites*

1. Puree the berries in a blender (for example redcurrant or raspberry will do fine). Heat up water or wine and pour in the sugar, stir until the sugar is dissolved. Let the mixture cool down and add some berries.

2. Beat the egg whites until they form stiff peaks and stir them carefully into the berry mixture.

3. Place the sorbet in the freezer (preferably in a stainless steel bowl) and stir carefully every half hour until the consistency is even. Cover and refreeze until serving time.

ENVIOUS NEIGHBOR
FLAPJACK WITH RICE

Serving 8 piglets:

- *6 eggs*
- *2 cups of milk*
- *3/4 cup of sugar*
- *1 1/2 teaspoons of salt*
- *1 cup of flour*
- *1 3/4 cups of rice pudding*
- *2 teaspoons of either vanilla flavored sugar or cardamon*

1. Preheat the oven to 400°F. Break the eggs into a bowl. Add the other ingredients and mix them well together. (If you don't have rice pudding, use flour instead. In that case, don't use cardamon. It works best with rice.)

2. Put parchment paper on a 9x12-inch baking tray and pour the mixture on it. Bake for 30 minutes. It will deflate dramatically when you remove it from the oven. Serve warm with whipped cream.

SHAKEN, NOT STIRRED
BÉARNAISE SAUCE

Four servings:

- 3 tablespoons of minced shallots
- 1/4 cup of white wine vinegar
- 1 tablespoon of minced or dried chervil
- 1 1/2 teaspoons of minced or dried tarragon
- 1 1/2 teaspoons of minced or dried parsley
- 1/4 cup of white wine
- 1/2 pound of butter
- 1/2 bay leaf
- 5 egg yolks
- salt

1. Place the shallots, chervil, tarragon, parsley and bay leaf as well as the white wine vinegar and white wine in a saucepan.

2. Simmer over low heat for 10 minutes. Pour the broth through a sieve, leaving about 1/3 cup of broth. Discard the solids.

3. Place the egg yolks in a stainless steel bowl with a round bottom and whisk in the broth. Put some water in a saucepan and bring to a low simmer.

4. Place the stainless steel bowl on the saucepan. Stir carefully until the mixture starts to settle and it doesn't taste like raw yolk anymore.

5. Whisk the chilled butter into the mixture in small pats. Season with white pepper and salt, if necessary. Add some chopped parsley, tarragon and chervil on top. Serve with steak or with grilled/fried salmon.

AND AGAIN AN OMELET
BAKED OMELET

Serves two pigs:

- *4 eggs*
- *1/4 cup of sour cream*
- *1/2 teaspoon of salt*
- *1 tomato*
- *1 green onion*
- *1/4 cup of cheddar or Swiss cheese*

 Preheat the oven to 325°F. Peel the tomato and cut it into half-inch pieces. Slice the onion and shred the cheese.

 In a bowl, beat the eggs, sour cream and salt for one minute. Stir in the tomato, onion and cheese.

 Pour the mixture into a buttered 8-inch pie pan. Bake uncovered until omelet has set and the top has a nice golden-brown color. This should take about 40 minutes. Serve immediately.

I'LL BE BACK
OVEN-MADE MINI OMELETS

Serves eight dieting pigs:

- *2 shallots*
- *oil*
- *butter*
- *6 eggs*
- *1/4 cup of cream*
- *1/2 teaspoon of salt (optional)*
- *black pepper*
- *3 1/2 ounces of smoked salmon*
- *2 tablespoons of grated Parmesan cheese*

1. Dice the shallots and fry them in oil until they are golden brown. Generously butter eight cups of a muffin pan. In a bowl, whisk the eggs and cream together. Mix with the fried shallots. Season with black pepper and salt. Divide the mixture evenly into the muffin cups.

2. Cut the smoked salmon into small pieces and sprinkle onto the omelets. Sprinkle grated cheese on top. Bake for 10 to 12 minutes in 350°F. The omelets should be left slightly soft in the middle. Serve with chopped fresh parsley.

TWISTED SPRING
HOLLANDAISE SAUCE

Four servings:

- 5 egg yolks
- 1 pound of butter
- 1/4 to 1/2 cup of lemon juice
- white pepper
- cayenne pepper

1. Place the egg yolks in a stainless steel bowl with a round bottom. Put some water in a saucepan and bring to a low simmer.

2. Place the stainless steel bowl on the saucepan. Stir constantly with a whisk for about 3 to 5 minutes until the mixture thickens enough to coat the back of a spoon.

3. Reduce the heat to low. Whisk the chilled butter into the mixture in small pats. Season with salt, pepper, cayenne pepper and fresh lemon juice. Add lemon juice until the sauce doesn't taste too greasy and has a nice fresh aftertaste.

4. Best serving temperature is 105°F to 175°F (otherwise it starts very soon to resemble scrambled eggs). When used to cover a dish, use 1/5 less butter. Serve with asparagus, vegetables or with steamed fish.

KARATE EGG
EGG SUSHI

36 sushi rolls:

- 6 nori sheets
- 2 cups of sushi rice
- 2 tablespoons of rice vinegar
- 2 tablespoons of sugar
- 1 tablespoon of salt
- 4 cups of water
- 6 eggs, beaten
- 1/4 cup of basil pesto
- salt and pepper to taste

 1. Pour the water in a saucepan and add the rice. Bring to a boil, reduce heat to low and cover. Cook for 20 minutes or until tender and water is absorbed. Let stand for 10 minutes. Combine the rice vinegar, sugar and salt in a small bowl and heat in the microwave on high for 30 to 45 seconds. Then fold the mixture into the cooked rice being sure to coat each grain. Place the rice in another bowl and let cool completely.

 2. Heat a skillet over medium heat and add a little bit of oil/butter before pouring in the eggs. Scramble until cooked through. Season with salt and pepper. Remove from heat and set aside.

3. Lay one nori sheet on a sushi mat, glossy side down. With wet hands, press a layer of rice about 1/3-inch thick onto the nori leaving about 1/4-inch of nori uncovered at the top and bottom edge. Spread a 1/2-inch wide line of pesto across the side nearest to you, leaving about 1 inch of rice uncovered at the bottom. Top with a line of egg. Begin with the edge of the mat nearest to you. Roll the mat up and over the ingredients so the ends of the mat and the nori meet.

 4. Cut the roll into 8 pieces with a sharp, wet knife. Don't serve the unaesthetic end pieces.

4. Cook the onions in the hot oil. Add ginger, garlic and tomatoes. Add the ground seed mixture, chili powder and ground coriander into the onion mixture and cook until the tomatoes are soft. Add water, coconut milk, palm sugar, tamarind and salt.

 5. Stir and cook until the mixture thickens (for about 7 minutes). Add the eggs and allow to simmer for 10 minutes. If the gravy is too thick, thin it out with some water. Serve with a proud smile!

SKILLED SKILLET
EGG AND HASH BROWNS

Serves four pigs:

- *6 eggs*
- *6 slices of veggie or turkey bacon*
- *2 cups of refrigerated hash browns*
- *1/2 medium onion, chopped*
- *1 1/2 cups of shredded Monterey Jack and cheddar cheese blend*
- *salt and pepper*

1. Cut the bacon into 1-inch pieces and fry up in a deep skillet until nice and crisp. Remove and leave enough bacon drippings to coat the bottom of a pan (add some melted butter if necessary).

2. Place hash browns in the pan, distribute evenly and top with chopped onions. Cook until the bottom is browned and flip over to cook all potatoes and onions. Pat into pan to form crust.

3. Beat the eggs in a bowl until fluffy and add 1 cup of cheese. Pour the seasoned mixture evenly over the potato crust in the pan. Cover with bacon pieces. Cover with a lid and let the eggs cook through. Add the extra cheese and let it melt before serving.

DAS EI
REAL EGG ROLL

Serves 12 piggies:

- *12 eggs*
- *1 cup of white sugar*
- *1/4 teaspoon of salt*
- *2 teaspoons of vanilla extract*
- *a dash of ground nutmeg*
- *6 cups of milk*

1. Mix the eggs in a bowl and stir in sugar, salt, vanilla and nutmeg. Heat the milk in a large saucepan until almost boiling, then slowly stir in the egg mixture. Whisk constantly to avoid scorching! Continue stirring as the mixture starts to thicken. After 15 minutes, curds start to form which look lumpy like oatmeal. Reduce the heat, stir occasionally for 5 minutes until some of the moisture is absorbed.

2. Place a cheesecloth over a large colander and pour the lumps and liquid (curds and whey) onto it. Lift the cheesecloth out and squeeze to remove as much liquid as possible. Tie the cloth tightly forming a sausage and let it hang for 3 hours. Cover with a damp linen and leave in refrigerator for 24 hours. Remove linen & cloth, slice to serve.

THE KING'S BREAKFAST
EGGS BENEDICT

**Serves one King or
up to four minions:**

- 4 fresh English muffins
- 8 slices of turkey
- 8 eggs
- salt and pepper
- Hollandaise sauce
  (see instructions on page 44)

 **1.** Preheat a griddle over medium heat and slice enough turkey to cover the muffins.

2. Start poaching the eggs (see instructions on page 51). Heat up the turkey slices on the griddle. Split the muffins in half and place the halves on the griddle, too.

3. Cook until the turkey is crispy enough and the muffins have been lightly toasted, butter the muffins generously and put them on a warm plate. Place the crispy turkey slices on top of the muffins.

 4. Place the drained poached eggs on top of the turkey. Add the warm Hollandaise sauce and/or spices on top of each egg. Serve immediately.

HOTTIE
CHILI PEPPER CASSEROLE

Serves four hungry pigs with moustaches:

- 4 ounces of peeled green chili peppers
- 8 ounces of shredded cheddar cheese
- 2 eggs
- 1 cup of milk
- 1/2 cup of buttermilk baking mix

1. Preheat the oven to 350°F and grease a 5-cup casserole dish. Remove seeds from peppers and rinse. Place peppers in a single layer and sprinkle cheese on top.

2. In a bowl, beat eggs thoroughly. Then beat in the milk and baking mix.

3. Pour mixture on the cheese and peppers. Bake for about 35 to 45 minutes until golden brown.

THE DIRTY DOZEN
PICKLED EGGS

- *12 eggs*
- *1 part vinegar*
- *1 part beet juice (from a jar of pickled beets)*
- *4 small celery sticks, salt, black peppercorns, sugar to taste*

1. Hard boil the eggs (see instructions on page 17) and peel them. Put the eggs into a pickle jar (12 eggs per jar) and fill the jar with vinegar and beet juice. Add the celery sticks, salt, black peppercorns and sugar. Close the jar and place it in the refrigerator.

2. In one day the eggs will start to be pickled. In three days they will be pickled right down to the yolk. To ensure your snacks' freshness, eat them within two weeks.

RAGNARÖK
PASTA & EGG SKILLET

Two pigs who are happy to eat anything after a hard day:

- *7 ounces of shell pasta, cooked, drained*
- *2 cups of cottage cheese*
- *1 teaspoon of dried marjoram leaves*
- *2 cups of frozen broccoli, cauliflower and carrot vegetable blend (defrosted)*
- *4 eggs*
- *salt and black ground pepper to taste*

1. Preheat a large non-stick skillet over medium heat and coat with cooking spray. Combine the pasta, cottage cheese and marjoram in the skillet and toss to coat evenly. Add the defrosted vegetables, toss to mix.

2. Cook for 5 to 10 minutes, stirring occasionally, until mixture is heated through and begins to sizzle. Use the back of a spoon to press four 2-inch diameter indentations into the mixture to make space for eggs. Break an egg in each indentation. Add salt and black ground pepper to taste.

3. Cover and cook over medium heat for 5 to 7 minutes until whites are completely set and yolks begin to thicken but are not hard. Cut in even portions (2 or 4) and serve.

NOODLE-DI-DOO
NOODLE-CRUSTED QUICHE

Serves four fast eaters:

- *3 cups of fine egg noodles, cooked, drained*
- *1 tablespoon of water*
- *1 cup of chopped green bell pepper*
- *3 tablespoons of chopped onion*
- *1 cup of chopped cooked ham*
- *6 eggs*
- *1 cup of milk*
- *1 tablespoon of prepared mustard*
- *salt and pepper to taste*

1. Preheat the oven to 375°F. Take a 9-inch pie plate, grease well and press noodles evenly on the bottom and sides.

2. Boil water in large non-stick skillet over medium-high heat. Add bell pepper and onion. Cook and stir until water has evaporated and vegetables are crisp-tender (3 to 4 minutes). Then add the ham and mix well. Spoon into the noodle crust.

3. Beat the eggs, milk and mustard in a bowl until fully blended. Carefully pour the mixture on top of the ingredients in the pie plate. Bake in the center of the oven for 30 to 40 minutes until center is puffed and a knife inserted near the center comes out clean. Remove from the oven and let cool down for 5 minutes before serving.

IT'S PARTY TIME!
VIRGIN EGGNOG

Serves eight under-aged piggies or four designated drivers:

- 4 eggs*
- 1/3 cup of sugar
- 2 cups of whole milk
- 1 cup of heavy cream
- 1 teaspoon of nutmeg
- 1 teaspoon of vanilla

1. Separate the egg yolks from the egg whites. Take the egg yolks and beat them until they lighten in color. Add the sugar to the mix and continue to beat until the sugar is completely dissolved.

2. Take a large saucepan and whisk together milk, cream and nutmeg over medium heat until ingredients are combined. Boil – stirring occasionally. Remove from heat, stirring constantly. Gradually add the milk mixture into the egg mixture until well combined.

3. Pour mixture into a saucepan and add the vanilla. Cook over medium heat, stirring until mixture reaches 160°F. Transfer to a large bowl, cover with plastic wrap and store in the refrigerator until chilled.

4. Before serving, place egg whites in a bowl and beat until stiff peaks form. Whisk egg whites into the eggnog and serve with a sprinkle of freshly grated nutmeg.

*RAW EGG WARNING!

EGGSTRAS

POINTLESS ACTIVITIES

CHEERS!

This is something you can play at a party or get-together. Supply everyone with a hard-boiled egg. The idea is for two people at a time to "toast" by raising their eggs and tapping them against each other. The one with the uncracked shell continues the game.

This toasting goes on until the very end when only one egg is left uncracked. The winner gets – well, a hard-boiled egg (with the uncracked shell), and a diploma for being the Egg Master of the Universe or the Sole Survivor of the Egg Bang.

SPOON ME

This is a great party game: carrying eggs with spoons! Set up a short course – maybe simply around a dinner table by removing all obstacles.

Give all participants a tablespoon and an egg (raw eggs make this game much more enjoyable). Everyone should place the spoon handle in their mouth and place the raw egg on the spoon. And off you go!

The first one navigating the entire course without dropping the egg is the winner and should be rewarded accordingly.

CATCH 'EM IF YOU CAN

If you get really bored or want to challenge yourself (or amuse yourself by getting some relatives involved), try to throw and catch a RAW egg! After a few practice throws, you might want to step it up a notch and try this technique: each time your partner catches the egg, take a step backwards before throwing it again and vice versa.

Throw the egg by using the underarm technique (not like a baseball!) by swinging your hand from the back to the front in one big sweeping motion. Try to land the egg exactly in the catchers' hands (who should be keeping his better hand palm upwards). Once he/she catches the egg, the arm movement has to continue backwards, otherwise the egg will break. This is due to the momentum of the egg yolk from the power of the throw.

BLOW IT OUT!

Eggs are also great to paint on if you don't have a canvas around or if you like to decorate your house for Easter. The egg shape is in fact what painters use when drawing human faces. The normal procedure is to paint cooked eggs, but you can also empty them so that your decorations last longer (after all, who wants smelly eggs laying around for months).

Here's how it goes down:

1. Take a raw egg.

2. Puncture both ends with a needle.

3. Blow into one of the holes.

4. The egg white & yolk come out of the other hole, so please place a bowl/glass underneath the egg if you don't want to make a mess – or if you want to use the ingredient for some useful purpose.

MASTER EGG CRACKER

Knowing how to properly crack an egg is a very sought after skill and it looks cool – you get bonus points from the opposite sex *and* it dresses you in the shining armor of a master chef capable of practically anything! Yes, it's the secret trade of the one-handed egg crackers. Besides all the benefits mentioned above, cracking an egg with one hand is also an effective way of making sure you get only one egg yolk in your cocktail as intended.

Take the egg in your "dominant" hand, i.e. a right-handed person in their right hand, and crack the eggs' longer side against the edge of a glass or bowl. After a few tries you will learn the right amount of strength necessary to break the shell but not end up bashing the egg into a pulp. Pull the egg shell halves apart by widening your fingers. Drop the egg yolk and white into the desired places.

EGG BEAUTY

GOLDIE LOCKS
HAIR MASK

If you have dry, dull, damaged, brittle, coarse or frizzy hair that looks like a lifeless raccoon on the side of the road, here's a great natural, chemical-free hair mask treatment just for you.

Break three eggs into a bowl and whisk them together, simultaneously adding three tablespoons of water. Apply the mixture to your hair evenly. Wrap your hair with plastic wrap or wear a shower cap for 10 to 15 minutes and let your body warmth do the trick. Take the cap off and let the eggs dry in your hair completely. Rinse your hair with warm water and then wash it with gentle shampoo. Now get out there and show your new hair to your envious neighbors!

HAIR MAGIC
HAIR GEL FOR MULLET & MOHAWK

Whisk two eggs, and add two tablespoons of water and one cup of sugar. Mix well. Use as hair gel by taking some of the mixture in your hand and rubbing it into the hair. Form to your liking.

SCALPATOL
SCALP CLEANING

Have you been avoiding dark colours recently for a reason? Dandruff is easy to get rid of. Break three eggs in a bowl and whisk them well while adding 1 teaspoon of water. Add ten drops of lemon juice for a nice smell and mix well. Scoop the mixture with your hands and massage it into the scalp. Let it dry completely for 10 minutes. Wash out with warm water and gentle shampoo. Go ahead and wear those black clothes again!

CANNONBALL
SKIN CARE FOR BALD HEADS

Take one egg and whisk it well. Use a pastry brush to cover the bald part of the head like you would do with a pastry. Let dry for a few minutes. Don't peel it off – the head will glisten in the sun like a beautiful wet stone on a sunny beach.

SKINNY VINNY
FACIAL MASK

Trouble with dry skin? No more! Take one egg and separate the yolk and egg white. Beat the yolk in a bowl and whisk until it's frothy. Apply the yolk to your face with a cotton pad as evenly as possible. Let dry completely. Wash off with warm water and gentle soap. Your skin will be glowing and gentle to the touch.

FAKE IT
EYE CARE

After not sleeping too well, you might have eye bags or the area underneath the eye may be slightly darker than normal. Here's a good tip to get rid of them: Take a boiled egg that has been in the refrigerator and press it on that area. Also, if you have a black eye, don't use a raw steak! Just peel a boiled egg and press the soft (and cool!) egg against the sore tissue. If you have a left-over omelet lying around in the fridge, that will do fine, too.

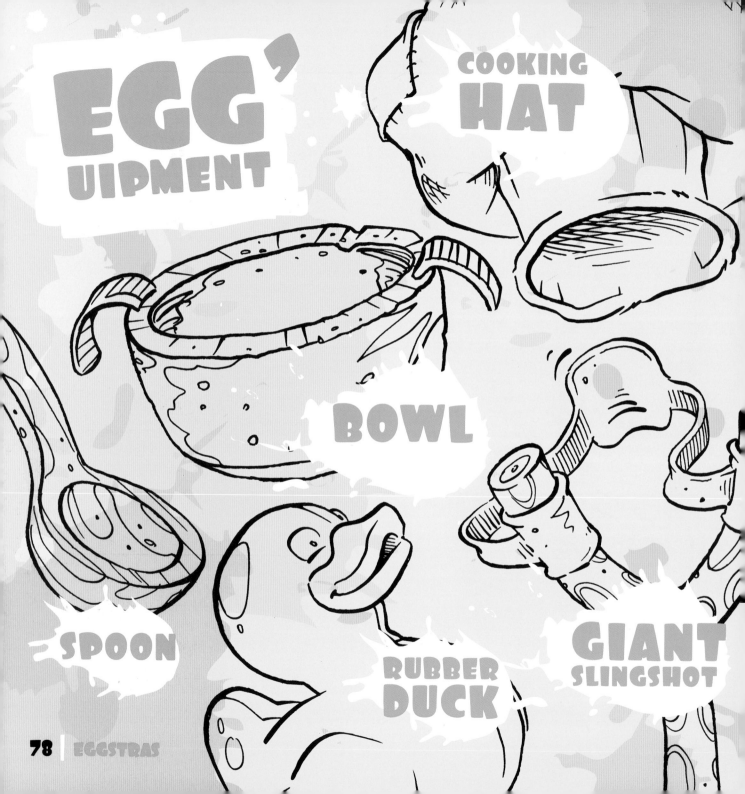

PLATE

SALT SHAKER

LOG

DONUT

TOASTER

ANGRY BIRDS COOKBOOK

EGG BASICS

Many species lay eggs, including birds, reptiles, amphibians and fish. Basically bird and reptile eggs have a protective shell and the inside consists of an egg white and yolk (and some membranes).

It should be rather clear to all that there are no Angry Birds eggs in the shops. Or at least they are not sold under that name (maybe the shopkeepers are afraid of the revenge of the birds!). Thus all recipes in this book are based on the use of regular chicken eggs.

Eggs are used in a wide range of foods. They can be cooked (hard and soft), scrambled, pickled, refrigerated and fried – or even eaten raw. As an ingredient, eggs are great for baking since the proteins in the egg white allow it to form foams and aerated dishes.

There is a variety of eggs to choose from coming in different sizes and from a wide range of producers. Every country has its own legislation and regulations regarding both food and health. Please choose eggs that are certified to be organic and laid by cage-free chicken.

Please note that eggs are a great source of protein, but they also contain a lot of cholesterol, fat, etc. Thus excessive consumption of eggs can't be good for your health, but within normal parameters, protein is a typical part of every nutritional diet.

RAW EGG WARNING! Please use caution in consuming raw and lightly cooked eggs due to the slight risk of salmonella or other food-borne illness. To reduce this risk, we recommend you use only fresh, properly refrigerated, clean grade A or AA eggs with intact shells, and avoid contact between the yolks or whites and the shell.

CONVERSION CHART

EQUIVALENTS

Fahrenheit	Celsius
300°F	150°C
325°F	160°C
350°F	175°C
375°F	190°C
400°F	200°C
425°F	220°C
450°F	230°C

For convection ovens, lower the temperature setting by 10°C/50°F (at all temperatures).

U.S.	Metric
1/8 teaspoon	0,5 ml
1/4 teaspoon	1 ml
1/2 teaspoon	2 ml
1 teaspoon	5 ml
1 tablespoon	15 ml
1 oz	3 cl
1/4 cup	60 ml
1/3 cup	80 ml
1/2 cup	120 ml
2/3 cup	160 ml
3/4 cup	180 ml
1 cup	240 ml
1 quart	1 liter
1/2 inch	1,27 cm
1 inch	2,54 cm

WEIGHTS AND MEASURES

3 teaspoons	1 tablespoon
4 tablespoons	1/4 cup
5 1/3 tablespoon	1 cup
8 tablespoons	1/2 cup
10 2/3 tablespoons	2/3 cup
12 tablespoons	3/4 cup
16 tablespoons	1 cup
1 tablespoon	1/2 fluid ounces
1 cup	8 fluid ounces
1 cup	1/2 pint
2 cups	1 pint
4 cups	1 quart
2 pints	1 quart
4 quarts	1 gallon
1 quart	1 liter
1 ounce	28 g
1 pound	454 g

INDEX